BEST OF ENGLAND

Essential Travel Guide to England in 2022 and 2023, concise Guide to England's Culture and etiquette and Amazing Places to Visit

Ben Booth

All rights reserved. No part of this publication may be reproduced, distributed, or transmitted in any form or by any means, including photocopying, recording, or other electronic or mechanical methods, without the prior written permission of the publisher, except in the case of brief quotations embodied in critical reviews and certain other noncommercial uses permitted by copyright law.

Copyright © Ben Booth, 2022.

TABLE OF CONTENT

CHAPTER ONE: HISTORY AND OVERVIEW OF ENGLAND

CHAPTER TWO: CULTURE AND ETIQUETTE OF ENGLAND

CHAPTER THREE: WHAT TO AVOID IN ENGLAND

CHAPTER FOUR: TRANSPORTATIONS IN ENGLAND

CHAPTER FIVE: GUIDE TO ENGLAND CURRENCY

CHAPTER SIX: ECONOMY OF ENGLAND

CHAPTER SEVEN: AMAZING PLACES TO VISIT IN ENGLAND

CHAPTER EIGHT: BEST HOTEL TO VISIT IN ENGLAND

CHAPTER NINE: AMAZING FOOD ONE CAN FIND IN ENGLAND

CHAPTER TEN: WHY YOU NEED TO VISIT ENGLAND

"England is the paradise of individuality, eccentricity, heresy, anomalies, hobbies and humors."

CHAPTER ONE: HISTORY AND OVERVIEW OF ENGLAND

England, the largest member unit of the United Kingdom, occupies more than half of the island of Great Britain.

Outside the British Isles, England is sometimes erroneously thought identical to the island of Great Britain (England, Scotland, and Wales) and even to the whole United Kingdom. Despite the political, economic, and cultural heritage that has ensured the continuation of its name, England no longer formally exists as a governmental or political unit unlike Scotland, Wales, and Northern Ireland, which all enjoy varying degrees of self-government in domestic matters. It is unusual for institutions to function in England alone.

Notable exceptions include the Church of England (Wales, Scotland, and Ireland, including Northern Ireland, which have different branches of the Anglican

Communion) and sports organizations for cricket, rugby, and football (soccer). In many respects, England has apparently been swallowed inside the bigger bulk of Great Britain since the Act of Union of 1707.

Laced by big rivers and little streams, England is a rich region, and the generosity of its soil has sustained a strong agricultural economy for millennia. In the early 19th century, England became the epicenter of a global Industrial Revolution and soon the world's most industrialized nation. Drawing resources from every settled continent, cities such as Manchester, Birmingham, and Liverpool converted raw materials into manufactured goods for a global market, while London, the country's capital, emerged as one of the world's preeminent cities and the hub of a political, economic, and cultural network that extended far beyond England's shores.

Today the metropolitan region of London spans most of southeastern England and continues to serve as the financial capital of Europe and to be a focus of innovation particularly in popular culture.

One of the primary English features is variation within a restricted boundary. No location in England is more than 75 miles (120 km) from the sea, and even the furthest spots in the nation are no more than a day's travel by road or train from London. Formed from the union of small Celtic and Anglo-Saxon kingdoms during the early medieval period, England has long comprised several distinct regions, each different in dialect, economy, religion, and disposition; indeed, even today many English people identify themselves by the regions or shires from which they come—e.g., Yorkshire, the West Country, the Midlands—and retain strong ties to those regions even if they live elsewhere.

Yet similarities are more essential than these distinctions, many of which started to fade in the years following World War II, notably with the change of England from a rural into a heavily urbanized culture. The country's island location has been of critical importance to the development of the English character, which fosters the seemingly contradictory qualities of candor and reserve along with conformity and eccentricity and which values social harmony and, as is true of many island countries, the good manners that ensure orderly relations in a densely populated landscape.

With the loss of Britain's vast overseas empire in the mid-20th century, England suffered an identity crisis, and much energy has been devoted to discussions of "Englishness"—that is, not only of just what it means to be English in a country that now has large immigrant populations from many former colonies and that is much more cosmopolitan than insular but also of what it means to be English as opposed to British. While English culture draws on the civilizations of the globe, it is remarkably unlike any other, if difficult to name and describe. Of it, English author George Orwell, the "revolutionary patriot" who recorded politics and culture in the 1930s and '40s, commented in The Lion and the Unicorn (1941):

England is limited on the north by Scotland; on the west by the Irish Sea, Wales, and the Atlantic Ocean; on the south by the English Channel; and on the east by the North Sea.

England's geography is low in height yet, except in the east, seldom flat. Much of it consists of sloping slopes, with the highest altitudes being in the north, northwest, and southwest. This landscape is based on complicated underlying structures that generate elaborate patterns on England's geologic map. The oldest sedimentary rocks and some igneous rocks (in isolated hills of granite) occur in Cornwall and Devon on the southern peninsula, ancient volcanic rocks underlie sections of the Cumbrian Mountains, and the most recent alluvial soils cover the Fens of Cambridgeshire, Lincolnshire, and Norfolk. Between these areas lay bands of sandstones and limestones of diverse geologic ages, many of them relics of ancient times when considerable sections of central and southern England were buried below warm seas. Geologic pressures raised and bent part of these rocks to create the spine of northern England—the Pennines, which rise to 2,930 feet (893 meters) at Cross Fell. The Cumbrian Mountains, which contain the famed Lake District, reach 3,210 feet (978 meters) at Scafell Pike, the highest point in England.

Slate covers much of the northern section of the mountains, while massive beds of lava are found in the southern half. Other sedimentary strata have generated chains of hills ranging from 965 feet (294 meters) in the North Downs to 1,083 feet (330 meters) in the Cotswolds. The hills known as the Chilterns, the North York Moors, and the Yorkshire and Lincolnshire Wolds were smoothed into typical plateaus with west-facing escarpments during three separate glacial episodes of the Pleistocene Epoch (approximately 2,600,000 to 11,700 years ago) (about 2,600,000 to 11,700 years ago). When the last ice sheet retreated, the water level rose, drowning the land bridge that had linked Great Britain with the European continent.

Deep layers of sand, gravel and glacial muck left by the receding glaciers further changed the environment. Erosion by rain, river, and tides and subsidence in sections of eastern England subsequently changed the hills and the shoreline. Plateaus of limestone, gritstone and carboniferous strata are connected with significant coalfields, some persisting as outcrops on the surface.

The geologic diversity of England is starkly displayed in the cliff formation of its coastline. Along the southern coast from the old granite cliffs of Land's End in the far southwest is a sequence of sandstones of varied tints and limestones of different ages, culminating in the white chalk from the Isle of Wight to Dover. A variegated landscape of cliffs, bays, and river estuaries marks the English coastline, which, with its various indentations, is nearly 2,000 miles (3,200 km) long.

The Pennines, the Cotswolds, and the moors and chalk downs of southern England serve as headwaters for most of England's rivers. The Eden, Ribble, and Mersey originate in the Pennines, run westward, and have a short path to the Atlantic Ocean. The Tyne, Tees, Swale, Aire, Don, and Trent originate in the Pennines, flow eastward, and have a long path to the North Sea. The Welland, Nen, and Great Ouse originate near the northern fringe of the Cotswolds and discharge into the Wash estuary, which forms part of the North Sea.

The Welland river valley is part of the fertile agricultural region of Lincolnshire. The Thames, the longest river in England, also originates in the Cotswolds and drains a huge area of southern England. From the moors and chalk downs of southern England emerge the Tamar, Exe, Stour, Avon, Test, Arun, and Ouse. All run into the English Channel and in some circumstances assist to make a pleasant environment along the shore. England's biggest lake is Windermere, with an area of 6 square miles (16 square km), situated in the county of Cumbria.

In trips of just a few kilometers, it is possible to pass through a sequence of various soil structures—such as from chalk down to alluvial river valley, from limestone to sandstone and acid heath, and from clay to sand—each kind of soil containing its own species of plant. The Cumbrian Mountains and much of the southern peninsula have acid-brown soils. The eastern portion of the Pennines features soils ranging from brown piles of earth to podzols. Leached brown soils prevail across most of southern England. Acid soils and podzols exist in the southeast. Regional factors, however, are essential. Black soil covers the Fens in Cambridgeshire and Norfolk; clay soil predominates in the hills of the Weald (in East Sussex and West Sussex); and the chalk downs, notably the North Downs of Kent, are covered with a kind of hard, dark clay, with sharp angular flints. Fine-grained deposits of alluvium exist in the floodplains, while fine marine silt occurs along the Wash estuary.

Climate or Weather in England is as varied as the geography. As with other temperate marine zones, the averages are mild, ranging in the Thames river valley from around 35 °F (2 °C) in January to 72 °F (22 °C) in July; while the extremes in England vary from below 0 °F (−18 °C) to over 90 °F (32 °C). The Roman historian Tacitus noted that the climate was "objectionable, with frequent showers and mists, but no acute cold." Yet snow covers the upper mountains of England for 50 days every year. England is renowned as a wet nation, and this is definitely true in the northwest and southwest.

However, the northeastern and central areas get less than 30 inches (750 mm) of rainfall yearly and regularly suffer from drought. In portions of the southeast the annual rainfall averages just 20 inches (500 mm). Charles II considered that the English climate was the nicest in the world. This changeability of the weather, not just season by season but day by day and even hour by hour, has had a tremendous impact on English art and literature. Not for nothing has the Bumbershoot become the quintessential walking stick of the English gentleman.

England shares with the rest of Britain a diminished spectrum of vegetation and living creatures, partly because the island was separated from the mainland of Europe soon after much of it had been swept bare by the last glacial period and partly because the land has been so industriously worked by humans. For example, a significant loss of mature broad-leaved woods, particularly oak, was a consequence of the abuse of lumber in the iron and shipbuilding industries. Today just a tiny percentage of the English landscape is wooded. Broad-leaved (oak, beech, ash, birch, and elm) and conifer (pine, fir, spruce, and larch) trees dominate the landscapes of Kent, Surrey, East Sussex, West Sussex, Suffolk, and Hampshire. Important forests include Ashdown in East Sussex, Epping and Hatfield in Essex, Dean in Gloucestershire, Sherwood in Nottinghamshire, Grizedale in Cumbria, and Redesdale, Kielder, and Wark in Northumberland.

A considerable percentage of England's forestland is privately owned. Vegetation patterns have been further affected via overgrazing, forest removal, reclamation and draining of marshlands, and the introduction of alien plant species. Though there are fewer species of plants than on the European mainland, they still cover a broad spectrum and include several rarities.

Certain Mediterranean species thrive in the protected and practically subtropical valleys in the southwest, while tundra-like vegetation is found in areas of the moorland of the northeast. England enjoys a plethora of summer wildflowers in its fields, lanes, and hedgerows, albeit in some parts they have been severely diminished by the use of herbicides on farms and roadside verges.

Cultivated gardens, which include various types of trees, shrubs, and flowering plants from throughout the globe, account for much of the diversified vegetation of the nation. Mammal species such as the bear, wolf, and beaver were eradicated in historic times, while others such as the fallow deer, rabbit, and rat have been introduced. More lately birds of prey have suffered at the hands of farmers safeguarding their sheep and their game birds. Protective measures have been taken, including a rule limiting the gathering of birds' eggs, and some of the less common species have started reestablishing themselves. The bird life is exceptionally diversified, largely because England is along the path of bird migrations. Some birds have found urban gardens, where they are routinely fed, to be a desirable habitat, and in London, approximately hundred different species are documented yearly. London also has a setting favorable to foxes, who in small numbers have colonized woodlands and heaths within a short distance of the city core. There are few varieties of reptiles and amphibians about half a dozen species of each but they are virtually all numerous where circumstances favor them.

Freshwater fish are abundant; the char and kindred species of the lakes of Cumbria presumably reflect an old group, linked to the trout that went to the sea before the geological upheavals that generated these lakes shut off its exit. Marine fishes are plentiful in species and in absolute numbers. The tremendous variety of shorelines creates habitats for various sorts of invertebrate creatures.

CHAPTER TWO: CULTURE AND ETIQUETTE OF ENGLAND

There are no particular etiquette norms that you have to abide by whilst in the UK. It is advisable, however, to display appropriate manners and respect for the local culture and customs.

The first, and most essential, step to British etiquette is to be aware of the obviously separate nationalities which compose the UK. The United Kingdom of Great Britain and Northern Ireland comprises England, Scotland, Wales, and Northern Ireland. The citizens of any of these nations are British. This phrase is also the safest to use when not certain about a person's ancestry. When assured of ancestry, you are permitted to name the various residents as follows: English, Scot, Welsh or Irish. While the four nations share many customs, each has its own set of traditions and history.

Greetings and meetings

When initially meeting a Brit, he or she may look reserved and icy, but that is simply an impression. In truth, they are really kind and helpful to tourists. A handshake is the standard method of greeting, but try to avoid extended eye contact, since it may make people feel ill at ease. Use last names and suitable titles unless expressly encouraged to use first names. It is normal to shake hands with everyone you know, regardless of gender; the acceptable answer to an introduction is "pleased to meet you".

Time and punctuality in British etiquette

British folks are highly severe when it comes to punctuality. In Britain, individuals make a considerable effort to appear on time, thus it is disrespectful to be late, even by a few minutes. If you are late, make careful to tell the person you are meeting. Here are several occasions where you are obligated to be on time, as well as other situations when it is advisable:

For formal dinners, lunches, or appointments you always appear at the precise hour set. For public meetings, plays, concerts, movies, sports events, courses, church services, and weddings, it's ideal to arrive a few minutes early.

You may attend any time throughout the hours mentioned for teas, receptions, and cocktail events.

The British regularly utilize terms such as "drop in anytime" and "come see me soon". However, do not take them literally. To be on the safe side, always telephone before visiting someone at home. If you get a written invitation to an event that states "RSVP", you should reply to the sender as quickly as possible, whether you are intending to attend or not.

Body language and clothing code

British folks are not too fond of exhibiting love in public. Hugging, kissing, and caressing are mainly for family members and really close friends. You should also avoid talking loudly in public or going to extremes with hand gestures throughout the course of the dialogue. The British enjoy a certain amount of personal space. Do not stand too close to another person or put your arm over someone's shoulder.

When it comes to attire, there are no boundaries and constraints on how to wear it. Just be sure that you observe the main principles while in formal circumstances. Observation will indicate that individuals in bigger cities dress more formally, notably in London. Men and women use wool and tweeds for informal situations. Slacks, sweaters, and jackets are ideal for men and women. Do not wear a blazer to work – it is a country or weekend dress.

On formal events, always choose an outfit that satisfies the dress code. When attending a holiday meal or cultural events, such as a concert or theatrical play, it is essential to dress formally.

Men should open doors for women and stand when a woman enters a room, however it is commonly acceptable for men and women both to hold the door open for each other, depending on who passes through the door first.

It is crucial to respect the British demand for privacy. Don't ask personal inquiries about family history and origin, occupation, marital status, political opinions, or money concerns. It is exceedingly courteous to breach a queue, therefore never push ahead in a line. It is also highly disrespectful to attempt to sound British or emulate their accent.

Remember that comedy is ever-present in English life. It is generally self-deprecating, mocking, sarcastic, sexist, or racist. Try not to take offense.

Cultural etiquette states that when welcomed to someone's house, you should offer a little gift to the hostess. Give flowers, chocolates, wine, champagne, or literature. Feel free to convey your thanks and joy for the visit on the following day with a message or a telephone call.

British etiquette guidelines for women

Women in Britain are entitled to the same respect and status as males, both in work and everyday life. The British have the inclination to use 'affectionate' terms while addressing someone, so do not take any offense if they call you love, dearie, or darling. These are regularly used and not considered disrespectful.

It is appropriate for a foreign lady to ask an English guy to supper. It is preferable to stick with lunch. Also, if you would want to pay for your lunch, you should express it at the beginning. Remember that while in public, it is normal to cross your legs at the ankles, instead at the knees.

Queuing

Supermarkets, railway stations, banks- you'll notice lineups wherever you go in the UK! British folks are quite disciplined when it comes to waiting in line patiently and anybody who attempts to skip the queue will undoubtedly get some unpleasant words or glances! However, most British people would cheerfully let you go ahead of them if you ask respectfully and have a legitimate cause.

Smoking

Cigarette smoking is quite popular in the UK. It's believed that one in six British people smoke. It's vital to understand that in 2007, smoking was outlawed in all enclosed public locations in England. This covers pubs, restaurants, and public transit. The University of Chester is a 'smoke-free' campus but does have approved smoking spaces. It's crucial to verify your lease agreement to discover whether smoking is permitted on your property.

Tipping

In the UK, tipping is prevalent and is the standard when it comes to dining in restaurants. Although you're under no duty to do so, adding a few more pounds to the bill is the customary procedure. There are no fixed recommendations on how much and when you should tip but this guide gives some helpful information.

Manners

International students frequently tell us how amazed they are by the courtesy of the British population. 'Please and thank you are undoubtedly some of the most popular expressions in the UK and it's crucial to say them when appropriate. British folks are likewise renowned for over-apologizing! You'll undoubtedly hear someone say sorry for a variety of little situations such as bumping into you or asking you a question. Spitting, passing wind, yawning/sneezing without covering your mouth, and littering should absolutely be avoided in public.

Greetings

The most prevalent form of greeting in the UK is a handshake. This is used when meeting someone for the first time and in formal events. Usually, you'll shake the other person's right hand with your right hand. Hugging and kissing on the cheek are normally reserved for welcoming close friends or family. Hello or hi are popular verbal greetings and you're also likely to hear 'alright?'- this also indicates hello and is not an inquiry.

Mobile phone etiquette

The majority of individuals in the UK have a mobile phone and social media plays a large influence in British society. Facebook, Twitter, and Instagram are quite popular and many individuals use WhatsApp to connect via text message. However, it's preferable to put your phone aside while chatting with someone or eating at the dinner table.

Tea

A cup of tea is a fundamental icon of British culture. You'll probably be served tea at most places you visit in the UK. Tea may also indicate your evening meal in the UK so bear this in mind. Breakfast, dinner, and tea or breakfast, lunch, and dinner are the most prevalent terms to describe meals.

British Humour

Sarcasm and being able to laugh at ourselves pretty much sums up British comedy. It may take a bit to get accustomed to this!

CHAPTER THREE: WHAT TO AVOID IN ENGLAND

English is one of the most unique countries in Europe. They persist in driving on the opposite side of the road, and they insist on using the pound even though they are members of the EU. There are many unique and weird things you will notice if you live here for a long or even if you only visit London for a short period. These are traditions that you will only see in England, and you will never see on the opposite side of the World.

The English adore queuing and they call it a queue instead of a line. In America, people stand in line, here they queue. You walk down to the tube (subway), and people are standing in an ordered line, waiting for the train to come.

If you attempt to skip the line, people will make really harsh remarks, and they will believe you are an arrogant foreigner, who doesn't respect the local traditions. So line jumpers will not be handled gently here.

Don't take up the full area on the escalator. Always stand on the right side of the escalator and allow others to pass by on the left side. If you take up too much space and you won't let others past you, you will hear the locals remarking on you.

Don't attempt to drink the English beneath the table, since you will lose. If you want to make English friends at a bar and you want to drink a couple of beers with them, that's wonderful. They are pleasant folks, who will appreciate the notion, but don't attempt to keep up with them unless you want to wind up suffering alcohol poisoning. They can stand outside of the bars for hours and drink from early afternoon until late at night, and they can drink pint after pint, and they can still stand on their own feet.

Don't ever say anything nasty about the Queen or the present king of England. The English adore the Queen and they believe Her Majesty is the finest thing England possesses. I even heard some of them declare that England's economy would never be damaged by Brexit because they had the Queen. The Queen is on every pound currency, and she is revered like no one else in the World.

Don't call the entirety of the UK, England. Especially not, when you encounter Scots, Welsh or Northern Irish, since they will be very much insulted. Many of them resist being part of the UK, and they have strong national identities.

If you are in the South of England, don't attempt to start up conversations with strangers in public, since it is not a very normal thing to do and people will not understand it. They will think you are simply an oddball.

When someone asks how you are, never react negatively. Tell them you are fine and everything is going nicely. In this nation, you will have to fake it. People will not speak about terrible things and the English won't even know how to handle bad news.

Don't insist on cold beer or coke with heaps of ice. Do like the natives, simply drink it warm.

If you encounter a Britt, who wants to chat about the weather, do not attempt to talk about anything else. Go on and chat about the weather for as long as Britt wants. It's their favorite thing to do in this nation, and they can go on talking about it for half an hour.

In London, never make eye contact. Londoners will do everything to avert eye contact on a full train. They will feel quite embarrassed if you gaze into their eyes and attempt to establish eye contact or if you begin a conversation with a stranger in public.

CHAPTER FOUR: TRANSPORTATIONS IN ENGLAND

Despite its various attractions, England is a very tiny nation with great roads and a vast rail network so getting about isn't difficult, no matter what the season.

The first significant choice while visiting England is whether to go by own automobile or utilize the enormous public transit system. Having your vehicle means you can make the greatest use of time and visit isolated destinations, but rental and gasoline expenses may be pricey, and there are always traffic delays to worry about.

Public transport, which includes a dependable system of trains and coaches (buses), is typically the preferable alternative for moving about in the UK. Aside from London, England's city cores are highly walkable too.

Choose the train for speedy long-distance travel

For long-distance travel across England, trains are normally quicker and more pleasant than buses but are usually considerably more costly. The English tend to grumble about their trains, although roughly 85% operate on time (and the 15% that encounter delays largely hit commuters) and major stations are well-equipped, with highly friendly employees, a selection of food outlets, and great facilities.

The primary difficulty for train fans these days is the expense. If you delay reserving your ticket until the last minute, rates might be extortionately expensive, therefore it's always best to book as long in advance as you can. Sometimes purchasing two single tickets might be cheaper than buying a return.

About twenty different firms run rail services in England, while Network Rail manages lines and stations. For some travelers, the variety of multiple train operators might be perplexing at first, although information and ticket-buying services are usually centralized.

If you have to change trains or use two or more rail operators, you may still purchase one ticket, good for the complete trip. The major rail cards and passes are also accepted by all train companies – and may provide substantial discounts.

Your first stop for arranging travel should be National Rail Enquiries, the country's comprehensive schedule, and ticket information service. The website promotes special discounts and contains real-time connections to station departure boards and downloadable maps of the train network.

You may also purchase tickets from the train companies directly, or via other ticket vendors, who frequently have easy-to-navigate websites; examples include Rail Easy and The Trainline. The ticket-splitting service Tickety Split is an excellent means of saving money on tickets, especially for one-way travel.

A National Express bus draws to a halt in London

Take the bus to lessen the burden on your budget

Long-distance buses are known as coaches in the UK, and services operate between most major towns and cities. If you're on a limited budget, coaches are virtually always the cheapest method to move throughout England, but they're also the slowest - often by a substantial margin.

If you book early or go during off-peak hours – preferably both – coach tickets may be quite inexpensive, however, if you're traveling to the airport then use a speedier train or cab for peace of mind that you'll make it in time for your flight. The two biggest coach companies are National Express and Megabus.

Tip for taking a coach: Many cities have different stations for local buses and long-distance coaches; make sure you travel to the proper one!

Hire a vehicle if you're traveling to isolated regions

Traveling by automobile or motorbike across England means you have more freedom and flexibility, and you can visit more isolated corners of the nation. Downsides for drivers include constant traffic congestion (even on freeways), the high price of gasoline, and the expense of insurance and parking fees in cities and tourist towns.

Compared with many nations (particularly the USA), car hire is pricey in England and petrol expenses may be eye-watering. The smallest automobiles start from approximately £130 (US 179) per week, while entry-level motorbikes cost £215 (US 296) per week. If you have time, utilizing a combination of rail, bus, cab, strolling, and sometimes riding a bike, you can travel to practically any place in England without needing to drive.

Tip for hiring a car: There are numerous large car-hire companies, but you may obtain a better price via a smaller firm nearby to your starting location, or go through a comparison site. Rental firms near airports may be fantastic for bargains, and they're simple to get through public transit, even if you're not traveling into a city.

Safe cycling for experiencing the beautiful outdoors

Hiring a bike – for an afternoon, a day, or a week or more – is a terrific way to truly explore a local location or experience

England's great outdoors. Some cities offer bike-share programs (as well as e-scooters), whereas others have longer-term bike-rental establishments. England also boasts a developing network of designated long-distance cycling routes that may encourage you to explore more of the nation by bicycle.

Bikes are commonly provided for rental at national parks or forestry areas, especially in regions utilized for leisure activities such as Kielder Water in Northumberland and Grizedale Forest in the Lake District. In certain regions, old railway tracks are now cycling trails, most notably routes in the Peak District in Derbyshire and the Bristol and Bath Railway Path in Somerset.

England is still a famously car-centric nation though, and most cities are not especially cyclist-friendly. Only a few cities have an appropriate system of dedicated bike lanes, so it's preferable to enjoy riding in more rural places, especially during the summer.

Flights are only worth it over long distances

England doesn't have a significant network of domestic aircraft owing to its small size, but several lengthy cross-country routes are unpleasant, expensive, and time-consuming if you go by rail (eg the journey from Exeter or Southampton to Newcastle).

However, you'll still spend at least £100 for one of these flights, and the time saved becomes less favorable if transit times and the travel to and from the airport are added in. England's local airline firms include British Airways, Loganair, FlyBe, EasyJet, and Ryanair, although, given the small distances and high carbon cost, many opt not to travel.

Hop aboard a boat to visit the Isle of Wight or Scilly Isles

The only significant ferry crossings inside England are from Portsmouth or Southampton to the Isle of Wight, and from Penzance to the Scilly Isles. If time isn't a problem, you may visit portions of England by canal boat; narrowboat hiring firms are centered around the Oxford Canal and the Grand Union Canal near Rugby.

Local buses and railways move you around and between towns and cities

English cities normally have strong public-transport networks – offered by a mix of buses, trains, and occasionally trams – but these services may be handled by a bewildering number of various businesses. There's generally excellent information at each stop or station, including route maps and ticketing information, and workers at tourist offices are often glad to assist.

Local bus services year-round in cities and towns save on Christmas Day and occasionally also on Boxing Day, when services either halt or operate on reduced schedules. Sundays also see fewer services. CityMapper is a great program for arranging the shortest travel between places, particularly if you're combining a transit alternative.

Buses operate in rural regions year-round, however, schedules are geared to serve schools and businesses, so there are fewer trips in the middle of the day and during weekends. Services may cease operating during summer school vacations, or buses may connect small villages to a market town just one day each week. It pays to do your study before going throughout rural England depending on bus transit alone.

In tourist locations (particularly national parks) there are frequently more frequent services from Easter to September. However, it's always good to double-check at a tourist office before organizing your day's activities around a bus that may not be operating.

How to grab a cab in England

There are two sorts of taxis in England - legal cabs with meters that may be hailed on the street, and "minicabs," which are cheaper but can only be ordered by phone. In London and certain other big cities, official taxi services are provided by the famed black taxis, which charge by distance and time. Ridesharing applications such as Uber are also an option in most towns and cities.

In remote locations, licensed taxis normally need to be booked by phone; search up the numbers for local taxi firms online as you plan your route, or enquire at a nearby bar or your hotel. You'll commonly find cabs waiting for fares at rural railway stations or a cab agency nearby.

Tip for getting a taxi: The Traintaxi website is a database that connects minicab companies with railway stations, letting you "bridge the gap" between the station and your ultimate destination.

Why I adore traveling by rail in England

The world's first commercial railway line ran between Liverpool and Manchester in 1830, but England post-war became increasingly car-centric, with unsightly motorways and drab ring roads spreading around the nation like wildfire. But I still adore the romanticism of train travel, and England's meandering lines are endowed with some stunning landscapes and fascinating history.

Trundling over the rolling green Chiltern Hills is the best way to reach London, while the stark dramatic vistas of the Yorkshire Dales will make you quickly put down your book or shut off your phone. Yes, English trains are prone to delays and don't have the airtight punctuality of places like Japan, but these rustic lines were trailblazers and you'll view much more of this nice, green area from a train window than from a freeway or from 35,000ft.

Take the magnificent sea-sprayed coastal line from Exeter to Dawlish and tell me you don't adore train riding!

CHAPTER FIVE: GUIDE TO ENGLAND CURRENCY

The UK unit of currency is pounds sterling (£), not the Euro. If you intend to visit Britain, it's necessary to educate yourself about UK money, particularly since new note and coin designs have been circulating between 2016 and 2018. Luckily, each note has a different color, so it is simple to distinguish them differently while you're searching through your wallet.

Currently, all of the banknotes and coins used in the U.K. include the portrait of Queen Elizabeth II. However, because of her recent demise, money will be updated with the new monarch, albeit it will take several years for the changes to be put into effect.

Fifty Pound Note

The 50-pound note has had various variations with paper notes portraying the first governor of the Bank of England, Sir John Houblon, and subsequently, Matthew Boulton and James Watt were portrayed on it. In 2021, a polymer 50-pound note was launched featuring a portrait of the legendary codebreaker, Alan Turing. Paper notes may be used until Sept. 30, 2022, at which time only polymer notes will be accepted by companies.

Twenty Pound Note

The Bank of England produced the Adam Smith 20-pound note in March 2007. The note displays Adam Smith, an 18th-century Scottish philosopher, and economist, on the back. It is the same size and largely the same color (purple) as the former 20-pound note that featured English musician, Sir Edward Elgar.

In 2020, a new 20-pound note showing legendary British painter JMW Turner entered circulation, replacing the Adam Smith piece. It will feature a self-portrait (the same 1799 picture that can be shown in London's Tate Britain museum), the ship represented in Turner's masterpiece The Fighting Temeraire, and the artist's phrase "light is, therefore, color" with his signature. Old paper 20-pound notes may be used until Sept. 30, 2022.

Ten Pound Note (Old)

The Bank of England 10 pound note is usually referred to as a "tenner." Old versions, such as the one depicted above, include Charles Darwin, who is famous for his theory of evolution and natural selection. The paper note featuring Charles Darwin was produced in 2000 and removed from circulation in March 2018.

Pound Note (New)

As of September 2017, a new yellow-orange 10-pound note has been released, portraying famed novelist Jane Austen. On the front, there is a new hologram with the crown, a see-through picture of Queen Elizabeth II, and Winchester Cathedral in gold foil. The other side contains a profile of Jane Austen, a Pride and Prejudice phrase, a picture of Elizabeth Bennet, and an image of Godmersham Park. This new bill is likewise plastic and waterproof.

Five Pound Note (Old)

This £5 note (sometimes termed a "fiver") was issued in 2001 and canceled in May 2017. It includes 19th-century jail reformer and philanthropist Elizabeth Fry. Known as the "angel of prisons," Fry fought for laws that supported humane treatment for detained people.

Five Pound Note (New)

Introduced in the Fall of 2016, the most current £5 note to go into circulation contains an image of Queen Elizabeth on one side and Sir Winston Churchill on the other. These vivid teal blue notes are purportedly cleaner and more difficult to counterfeit owing to new security measures. One concern with the new polymer notes is that they have a propensity to stick to one other from static electricity. So if you have multiple new ones, be sure you don't unintentionally pay with two notes instead of one.

UK Coins

There are eight recognized coins in UK money all of which are struck by the Royal Mint. The coins' values are 2 pounds, 1 pound, 50 pence, 20 pence, 10 pence, 5 pence, 2 pence, and 1 cent (penny). In 2008, the backs of all the pence coins were altered to depict various portions of the Royal Shield. Pound coins are occasionally referred to as "quids" by locals, so don't be confused if you hear that term on the street or in stores.

The slang phrase refers to the value rather than to the 1-pound coin itself. The phrase is not used for other coins except in terms of their worth. So, if you had a handful of mixed coins worth a total of 2 pounds you may say you had a couple of quids worth of coins.

Two-pound coin

The British 2-pound coin features a silver-colored center and gold-colored edge. Since it was launched in 1997, the 2-pound coin has had three distinct images of Queen Elizabeth II. The front was created by Jody Clark in 2015.

The reverse side of the 2-pound coin has likewise altered. Bruce Rushin created the first coin, which was circulated from 1997 until 2015. It displayed a collection of linked gears and the words "standing on the shoulders of giants" around its edge to reflect Britain's technological accomplishments from the Iron Age to the Industrial Revolution.

The newest coin, in circulation today, includes Antony Dufort's Britannia design with the motto "Quatuor maria video," which translates to "I shall claim the four seas."

Close-Up Of One Pound Coin

At first, the 1-pound coin may seem identical to the 2-pound coin. They both sport Jody Clark's Queen Elizabeth II design on the front and both are bimetallic. However, the new £1 coin, which was launched in March 2017, is 12-sided and has an entirely new design on the reverse. As a tribute to the United Kingdom's four countries, there is an English rose, a Scottish thistle, a leek for Wales, and a shamrock for Northern Ireland, all rising from the top of a crown. The currency is slated to undergo another makeover in 2023 with a design by Keyan-born British artist Michael Armitage.

Fifty Pence Coin

The 50 pence (50p) coin is a seven-sided, silver coin. Since it was initially designed in 1969, the coin has featured Queen Elizabeth's profile on the front.

Twenty Pence Coin

Twenty pence (20p) coins appear extremely similar to 50p coins in that they're both seven-sided, silver, and contain a picture of Queen Elizabeth II on the front and a section of the Royal Shield on the reverse. If you become confused, look out for the label ("20 pence" or "50 pence") on the back of each coin to separate them.

Ten Pence Coin

The 10 pence (10p) coin is circular and silver, featuring a picture of Queen Elizabeth II on the front and a section of the Royal Shield on the reverse.

Five Pence Coin

Five pence (5p) coins are comparable to 10p coins. They are both circular and silver, featuring Queen Elizabeth II on the front and a section of the Royal Shield on the reverse. However, the 5p coin is substantially smaller than the 50p, 20p, and 10p coins.

Two Pence Coin

Round two penny (2p) coins stand out since they are composed of copper. Otherwise, the design remains the same: Queen Elizabeth's image and a part of the Royal Shield.

One Pence Coin

The copper one pence (1p) coin is usually called a "penny." It is the lowest-value coin to be circulating in the UK.

CHAPTER SIX: ECONOMY OF ENGLAND

The economy of England was mostly agrarian until the 18th century, but the Industrial Revolution led it to transform gradually into a highly urbanized and industrial area throughout the 18th and 19th centuries. Heavy industries (iron and steel, textiles, and shipbuilding) flourished in the northeastern counties due to the closeness of coal and iron ore reserves.

During the 1930s the Great Depression and foreign competition led to a drop in the output of manufactured products and an increase in unemployment in the industrial north. The jobless from these northern areas went south to London and the neighboring counties. The southeast grew urbanized and industrialized, with an automobile, chemical, electrical, and machine tool makers as the dominant industries.

A rise in population and urban expansion over the 20th century caused a major decline in the acreage of farms in England, although the geographic counties of Cornwall, Devon, Kent, Lincolnshire, Somerset, and North Yorkshire have remained primarily agricultural.

Another era of economic decline throughout the late 20th century saw the virtual collapse of coal mining and severe employment losses in iron and steel production, shipbuilding, and textile manufacturing. The demise of these sectors severely harmed the economy of the north and Midlands, while the south remained reasonably affluent. By the beginning of the 21st century, England's economy was firmly dominated by the service sector, especially banking and other financial services, retail, distribution, media and entertainment, education, health care, hotels, and restaurants.

Agriculture, forestry, and fishing

The physical environment and natural resources of England are more suitable for agricultural growth than those of other areas of the United Kingdom. A bigger share of the land consists of lowlands with excellent soils where the climate is suitable for grass or crop production. The bulk of English farms are modest, most holdings being less than 250 acres (100 hectares). Nonetheless, they are extremely automated.

Major crops

Wheat, the major grain crop, is cultivated in the drier, sunnier areas of eastern and southern England. Barley is farmed largely for animal feed and malting and other industrial uses. Corn, rye, oats, and rapeseed (the source of canola oil) are also farmed. Principal potato-growing locations are the fenlands of Norfolk, Cambridgeshire, and Lincolnshire; the clay soils of Lincolnshire and East Riding of Yorkshire; and the peats of North Yorkshire. Sugar beet cultivation relies largely on government subsidies because of competition from imported cane sugar. Legumes and grasses such as alfalfa and clover are produced for feeding animals.

The cultivation of vegetables, fruits, and flowers, known in England as market gardening, is generally done in greenhouses and is situated within easy trucking distance of big cities, the closeness to a market being of greater concern than climatic considerations. The rich (clay and limestone) soil of Kent has long been suitable for fruit growth; their cultivation was first introduced on a commercial basis in the 16th century. Kent is a key provider of fruits and vegetables (apples, pears, black currants, cauliflowers, and cabbages) (apples, pears, black currants, cauliflowers, and cabbages). Worcestershire is known for its plums, whereas Somerset and Devon specialize in cider apples.

Livestock

The agriculture of England, while to a lower degree than in Wales and Scotland, is principally focused on cattle husbandry and, in particular, milk production. Dairying is significant in every county, however, the major concentrations are in western England. The English have a rich legacy of cattle breeding, which profited tremendously from better procedures following World War II. Higher-yielding dairy breeds, notably the Frisian and Ayrshire, have grown more prevalent than the once-dominant Shorthorn.

Domestic production meets most of the country's meat requirements. Special beef breeds, for which Britain is famed, are farmed across the nation, although long-established specialty regions maintain their significance. Cattle are routinely transferred from one location to another for rearing, storage, and ultimate fattening. The beef sector faced severe losses in the late 1990s due to fears about an epidemic of bovine spongiform encephalopathy ("mad cow disease").

The foot-and-mouth disease epidemic in 2001 had a terrible impact on the livestock business, requiring the killing of several million animals—mostly sheep but also cattle, pigs, and other animals—and generating major losses for agriculture. Although instances occurred in many sections of the nation, the epidemic was especially severe for Cumbria, where more than two-fifths of the cases occurred.

Hill sheep are raised in the Pennines, the Lake District, and the southern peninsula, locations where sheep are sometimes the principal source of a farmer's income but generally of secondary significance to cattle. The raising of lambs for meat rather than wool is the major preoccupation of English sheep producers. Grass-fed breeds, giving lean meat, are far more significant than the huge varieties, grown on the arable ground, that were distinctive of the 19th century.

While dedicated pig farms are uncommon, they do exist, serving the main sausage and bacon industries. Poultry is maintained in modest numbers on most farms, although specialized poultry farms, particularly in Lancashire and in the southeastern regions feeding the London market, have developed.

Forestry

Many kinds of wood in England are controlled by the Forest Commission, which, despite boosting timber production, also stresses wildlife protection. During the 18th and 19th centuries, wood was intensively utilized by the iron-and-steel and shipbuilding industries. Presently need for wood remains in the building and furniture sectors, but, with the government's afforestation program in operation, new coniferous forests are starting to dot the terrain.

Fishing

Freshwater fish, including bream, carp, perch, pike, and roach, are accessible in the rivers of eastern England. Cod, haddock, whiting, herring, plaice, halibut, turbot, and sole are taken in the North and Irish seas. Several ports, notably Lowestoft, Great Yarmouth, Grimsby, Bridlington, and Fleetwood, have freezing and processing operations nearby. Oyster farms are spread along the rivers and estuaries of Essex, while rainbow trout farming has grown popular. Salmon fishing is forbidden in seas greater than 6 miles (10 km) from the shores of England.

Resources and power

For much of the 19th and 20th centuries, coal was England's richest natural resource, supplying most of the nation's demand for energy. However, worldwide rivalry, increasing domestic prices, the rise of cheaper local alternatives (such as natural gas), and developing environmental concerns conspired to cripple the coal sector in the 1980s and '90s. Coal output is presently just one-fifth of its mid-20th-century level. New technologies and the discovery of vast amounts of petroleum and natural gas in the North Sea have further changed the structure of energy production. Natural gas provides the highest amount of England's energy demands, followed by oil, coal, and nuclear power.

Manufacturing

Sand, gravel, and crushed rock are commonly accessible and supply raw materials for the building sector. Clay and salt are abundant in northern England, while kaolin (china clay) is accessible in Cornwall.

About one-fifth of England's employees are involved in manufacturing. Major industries found in the northern counties include food processing, brewing, and the manufacturing of chemicals, textiles, computers, vehicles, airplanes, apparel, glass, and paper and paper products. Leading industries in southeastern England include pharmaceuticals, computers, microelectronics, aviation components, and autos.

Finance

Financial services are essential to England's economy, notably in London and the South East. A significant international headquarters for finance, banking, and insurance, London—especially the City of London—hosts such centuries-old organizations as the Bank of England (1694), Lloyd's (1688), and the London Stock Exchange (1773), as well as more recent entrants. Although London leads the industry, financial services are also prominent in other cities, such as Leeds, Liverpool, and Manchester.

Services

Service activities account for more than two-thirds of employment in England, partly because of the predominance of London and the prominence of the financial services industry. As the national capital and a recognized cultural destination, London also offers a great number of employment in government and education, as well as at its numerous cultural organizations.

The cities of Cambridge, Ipswich, and Norwich are key service and high-technology hubs, as is the "M4 corridor"—a group of towns, such as Reading and Swindon, along the M4 highway between London and South Wales. Retailing is robust across the nation, from ubiquitous local grocers to the exquisite boutiques of Mayfair in London's West End.

Tourism also plays a vital part in England's economy. The country's attractions appeal to a broad array of interests, ranging from its rich architecture, history, arts, and culture to its horticulture and gorgeous scenery. A huge percentage of England's domestic holidaymakers go for coastal places such as Blackpool, Bournemouth, and Great Yarmouth. The southern counties, with their huge coastline and national parks, also draw a considerable number of visitors. However, the seasonal and low-paid nature of many services and tourist-related occupations has kept the average wage lower in the southwest than in most other regions of England.

Millions of British and foreign visitors yearly visit London landmarks such as the British Museum, the National Gallery, Westminster Abbey, Saint Paul's Cathedral, and the Tower of London; even more, go outside the city to take in Canterbury Cathedral and York Minster.

CHAPTER SEVEN: AMAZING PLACES TO VISIT IN ENGLAND

The North York Moors, Yorkshire

This national park with a coastline comes with all the credentials: Yorkshire's wild and magnificent rolling hills, invaded by pastoral valleys such as those at Rosedale, replete with historic mine workings on the valley slopes. A vintage steam line clambers across the hills from Pickering to Grosmont, coughing and puffing as it goes. Whitby, a vibrant seaside village, is noted for its fish and chips, Dracula links, and ruined abbey. And then there's the coastal walk that goes from protected beaches to rugged headlands, with stunning vistas.

Grasmere and Ambleside, Cumbria

These two communities capture so much that is excellent about the Lake District. Grasmere, with its bijou spangle of water, is all genteel sumptuousness, with boutique shopping, excellent dining, and literary trips to Wordsworth's home.

Meanwhile more businesslike Ambleside, with its adventure outfitters, stands at the north end of boat-rich Windermere, the busiest and largest of the English lakes. A short hard trek up from here via rocky knolls to Loughrigg Fell provides an eyeful of everything, with breathtaking views of the serpentine length of Windermere and the Langdale Pikes.

Chatsworth and Haddon, Derbyshire

England's aristocratic rural estates stretch over a kaleidoscope of styles and eras. The Duke of Devonshire's Chatsworth House, for example, commanding its river valley inside the Peak District, is a splendid family-owned house making the most of its primarily 18th-century assets with tours, walks, and events. Meanwhile, a couple of valleys away, you can walk back a few centuries inside 13th-century Haddon Hall, one of the most wonderfully preserved medieval buildings in the UK, with its banqueting hall, Tudor-painted ceilings, and Elizabethan walled gardens.

Bath, Somerset

A location of Roman baths and Georgian crescents, the Bath stands cradled in hills in its little universe, a realm evocative of ball dresses and chatting aristocracy, as witnessed by Jane Austen. The creamy-gold Bath stone and honeycomb of Palladian-influenced terracing, rising in curved waves up the hillsides, are what makes the city so physically beautiful. Somehow a river and a canal weave through, and at the heart of the city lies the ancient thermal spa established by the Romans back in approximately AD75, with steam still coming from the hot spring.

Cotswold villages, Gloucestershire and Oxfordshire

Manor buildings with gurgling brooks and hamlets of honey-colored stone. Tea rooms abounding, artisan delicatessens, historic cathedrals, and Bibury, the hamlet that the artist William Morris regarded as "the most beautiful in England". This is the Cotswolds. Mind you, Bourton-on-the- Water must be a rival for the "most beautiful" label, too. Here the River Windrush runs over a spacious green, traversed by footbridges and bordered by attractive inns. Weeping willows trace their tresses in the water, ducks wait for chips and there's a toasted teacake around every turn.

Jurassic Coast, Dorset, and Devon

This Unesco-recognised length of the southern coastline begins at the eastern end of the eccentric town of Swanage, where the pillars of Old Harry Rocks overlook Poole Harbour. From here it stretches westwards, circling wild St Aldhelms Head, trampling through fossil-rich Kimmeridge, to the nearly perfect circle that is Lulworth Cove and the arch of Durdle Door.

Then, from Weymouth, the Chesil shingle scythes westwards towards the cliffs of Charmouth and West Bay, so famed for its crumbliness and their fossil dinosaurs. The Regency resort of Lyme Regis, beyond, is where The French Lieutenant's Woman was shot.

Helford and Roseland, Cornwall

You don't go to Cornwall for the towns — unless they've tucked up a stream or pouring onto a bay. It's the coast that matters, either the north for the wild and spectacular, or the south for the streams and headlands. Both sides have beaches to be proud of, but for shelter and history head for the south's Helford River, the scene for Daphne du Maurier's Frenchman's Creek.

East of Helford, the Roseland Peninsula starts with the wealthy fishing resort of St Mawes. In this section of Cornwall, the spring gardens of Trelissick and Caerhays are ablaze with magnolias and camellias far before the rest of the nation.

Norfolk coast, Norfolk

North Norfolk is like a watercolor picture, where land, sea, and sky appear to mix smoothly into one another. Migrating wildfowl add their thread to the sky above while seal colonies loll about on sandbanks like rolls of abandoned carpet. Towns such as Burnham Market, with its art galleries and excellent restaurants, are shockingly affluent — but then maybe that shouldn't be a surprise, considering that Holkham Hall, the house of the Earl of Leicester, and Sandringham, the Queen's country estate, are just inland.

Wye Valley, Herefordshire

Some claim British tourism originated back in 1745 on the lazy, peaceful river at Ross-on-Wye when the local rector took paying visitors out on boat journeys.

Today a lot of the watercraft activity has fallen southwards to Symonds Yat, a paradise for kayakers and for trekking its high wooded banks. Meanwhile, in Ross, the venerable old half-timbered frontages of the town stand back somewhat upward of the river, and it is largely cyclists that follow the stream, especially its prettiest length up beyond Hole-in-the-Wall, burrowing via back roads into Hereford.

Cambridge, Cambridgeshire

The flat fens of Cambridgeshire seem an unusual site for a seat of learning, yet the colleges and chapels of Cambridge live their magical universe, huddled around the banks of the somnolent River Cam. Unlike Oxford, which can be raucous and crowded, Cambridge is a site of robed folks emerging from old entrances and bumping away over cobbles on bicycles. To rent a punt and to glide softly down the so-called Backs (the backs of several universities) is to gain a look into a sophisticated, ageless world.

Rye and Romney Marshes, Kent and East Sussex

The historic town of Rye was formerly one of the Cinque Ports, five defensive ports in Kent, Sussex, and Essex described in Magna Carta and it looks to have scarcely altered, although the sea has since receded. The village is a lacework of galleries, patisseries, wisteria, and leaded windows. It rises strongly over Romney's old marshlands, now drained and striped with wheatfields. Beyond are the beautiful beaches of Camber Sands and the strange shingle coast of Dungeness, with its peculiar fishing fleet.

Test Valley, Hampshire

A network of crossing rural roads and the babbling gin-clear waters of some of the most expensive fishing rivers in England make this an exhilarating piece of the English countryside. Stretching approximately from the town of Hurstbourne Priors down to Romsey, this is a site to observe leisurely trout and gorgeous waterside houses. A location to fossick out classic pubs like the Mayfly or the Peat Spade, and historical sites such as the National Trust's Mottisfont Abbey, with its famed rose garden. Even Waitrose is here with its Leckford estate, featuring 4,000 acres of farming, fishing, and water gardens.

CHAPTER EIGHT: BEST HOTEL TO VISIT IN ENGLAND

The United Kingdom's biggest nation, England, has long been the inspiration of poets, playwrights and swashbuckling period. This lush and attractive area, smaller than many American states, packs a great punch: eleven national parks, elegant residences, and towns bursting with innovation.

It's a seductive environment suitable for exploration, and while the distances aren't great, it's simple enough to pong between the many regions which equally come with their own individuality.

Idle Rocks, St Mawes

You come to Cornwall for sea vistas and salt air, and this delivers in buckets and spades. Bang on the coast in St Mawes, it's extremely Cornish chic: fresh and zesty in mood, from the vibrant textiles in public spaces (rooms are in subdued pastels) to cheery young employees in chinos. It's the stance that sells it, however.

Yachts on the Fal estuary pass by as you drink cocktails on the patio, and at low tide, a pipsqueak beach emerges. Maps hanging on bedroom walls encourage you towards treks around the Roseland Peninsula, but you may find yourself lacking the drive to leave the hotel.

Blakeney Hotel, Norfolk

You'll book for the weekend and wish you had a week: while pushed up by its family owners, this 1920s boutique hotel on the port of Blakeney is as cozy as your favorite sweater. Rooms are pleasantly eccentric, wonderfully done in linens and marble. The finest have balconies – select 43, 47, 48, and 50 for the views, or choose G1 to G5 for the dog. Alongside an indoor pool and superb restaurant, amenities include a "lookout lounge" with views across the salt marsh; the best pick for neighboring Norfolk treks.

Middleton Lodge, North Yorkshire

This stylish boutique hotel on the edge of Swaledale is a delightful mix in God's own land — very much a rural stay (you're on a 200-acre walled estate), yet the design is bang up to date.

Relaxed style, which tends towards retro, fits comfortably beside rough stone and brick walls. Rooms differ depending on where you are on the estate: serene in the coach house, cool in the dairy, adorable in old gardeners' cottages. Five open onto a patio, while most feature clawfoot bathrooms. Life centers around a lovely restaurant - showing the vast Yorkshire larder — which extends onto the garden in summer.

Rectory Hotel, Cotswolds

There are some spectacular hotels in the Cotswolds countryside, but this is not one of them. Things have stayed wonderfully low-key at this 18-room boutique hotel in charming Crudwell town. It might be a home from home, where your own gaff is also a gorgeous country property merging Georgian characteristics with subtle contemporary comfort.

Rooms offer slipper bathtubs and wonderfully soft mattresses and are nestled among magnificent gardens - select number 11 for the greatest views. The restaurant is set in a light-filled glasshouse, or go to The Potting Shed, across, for top-notch pub fare.

Pig on the Beach, Dorset

A redesigned beach hotel, this higgledy-piggledy country house stands in an implausibly picturesque village with one of the greatest vistas on the south coast (Studland Bay is a three-minute walk away). Like other outposts of the Pig chain, this magnificent Dorset environment is ornamented with a hotel spa, sprinkled among dinky shepherds' huts (book ahead), and features a restaurant offering garden-to-plate meals. Its 23 romantic rooms soften the elegance with just the right amount of shabby: roll-top showers, reclaimed flooring, flora images on walls, and vistas to the sea.

Artist Residence, Brighton

Sassy and quirky, on a stylish Regency square, the Artist Residence beach hotel offers a concentrated dosage of Brighton as intoxicating as sea air. Local artists had a role in decorating rooms — they are all named after their founders — but owners Justin and Charlie were the leading spirits. They offer a seamless flair to the interiors with a mix-and-match of industrial and antique; a stylish art poster here, a butter-soft leather couch, or a slipper bath there. Room sizes vary from titchy to ordinary, and while street noise penetrates up to lower levels, you're unlikely to bother. You'll undoubtedly be immersed in the hotel Clubhouse – a stylish lounge, café, and cocktail bar that's an attraction in its own right.

The Pig in Harlyn, Cornwall

There are plenty of flashy coastal hotels in Cornwall, but few have the charm of this manor hotel behind a stunning shoreline south of Padstow. Though its listed Jacobean edifice creaks with history, its designers' superb eye has produced a stay steeped in a bohemian flare.

There are velvet couches and antique knick-knacks, oil paintings and vintage prints, brooding petrol-blue paneling and colorful wallpaper, as well as a line of Hunter wellies available to borrow at the entrance. Rooms are rustic and cool, with four first-choice "garden wagons" overlooking the vegetable patches and fields. Dining is all about being hyper-local, whether in the boho-glam restaurant or outside the lobster shack.

Another Place, Lake District

The developers behind Cornwall's renowned Watergate Bay hotel used the same concept here: simplified architecture that compliments, rather than upstages, the Lake District environment. Fells and water loom beyond every window; from those in the contemporary, family-friendly rooms (book a "best" room to secure unimpeded lake views) to those in the crisp restaurant. Perhaps the greatest view of all is the one from the 65ft infinity pool, its wall of glass facing Ulls water.

Head outdoors to take hikes close by, or on the estate's jogging paths or boats. Those who are courageous enough to join one of the hotel's guided wild swims may thaw out in the hot tub afterward, a particularly romantic area on a beautiful night.

The Mitre, Hampton Court

Why blow the budget on a central London hotel when there's equivalent quality, greater views, and more calm available at half the price, just 30 minutes away? Recent rehabilitation of this grade II listed old inn at Hampton Court, now a boutique hotel, has given extravagant design to pleasingly crooked rooms. The Catherine Parr suite receives top credit, but there are no duds. Cool but playful, it's like spending a night inside a Wes Anderson film. Public rooms open out to a magnificent patio, so on bright days, you may have breakfast by the river.

The Peacock in Rowsley, Peak District

What's not to enjoy about a good-value boutique hotel creaking with history? This is an exceptional Peak District stay in the 17th-century dower house of Haddon Hall estate. Modern chairs and lighting replace romantic rooms with mullion windows, beams, and antiques; request one at the back to prevent noise from the A6. Public rooms are all plush armchairs and ancient oils, the day's newspaper in the bar, and the subtle scent of wood smoke. The British restaurant is bang up to date, featuring beef and game from the estate, with seats extending beyond French windows to a patio. Go on hikes close by or catch your lunch: the grounds of Haddon Hall feature some of the greatest wild trout fishing in Britain.

Fritton Lakes, Norfolk

You want a hotel, the kids want an adventure vacation - here is the answer. Whether you stay in the clubrooms of the rural mansion belonging to owner Lord Somerleyton (Hugh Crossley), cottages, or the woods cabins (ideal for couples), the vibe is of a grown-up summer camp. Estate bar The Fritton Arms prides itself on its zero-food-miles cuisine, plus there are paddleboarding and swimming chances on the two-mile lake, and a floating sauna. The 1,000 acres are part of an ongoing rewilding initiative – red deer stalk the heath and birds flutter in copses, and there are plans to bring bison too.

Cliveden House, Berkshire

It's the hang-the-expense luxury hotel that's housed royalty, celebrities, artists, and politicos for generations, a location of such flair that Meghan Markle picked it as her pre-wedding stay. The historic manor home of the Astor family has belle époque romanticism in plenty.

Though decorated with antiques, big rooms named after renowned previous visitors are everything from faded, and the restored hotel spa is a Chanel commercial come to life. The 376-acre gardens are similarly lovely, with conker-shiny antique boats available for river rides.

The Traddock, Yorkshire Dales

Where most hotels do décor by numbers, this little country property in the Yorkshire Dales is all heart and soul, due to its family owners. Repeat customers (who comprise two-thirds of the clientele — usually a good indication) have preferences among its 12 rooms: classic in the doubles; a contemporary country in a deluxe room; or open-plan suites with rural vistas.

All are littered with antiques, as are public rooms, where you'll also discover fires in grates and flowery William Morris wallpaper. The garden outside is equally a treat - after you've rediscovered how to relax, there are hikes close by in the Dales and Forest of Bowland.

University Arms, Cambridge

This 19th-century pile didn't use to live up to its central Cambridge location near a park, but an £80 million makeover has restored its vintage grandeur. The aesthetic is formal British, with marble and brushed brass in suites that peer over the green, with a top coat of fun. Beyond porters in red coats and a lobby calling for a Hollywood actress are flashes of modest quirkiness, such as carpeting patterned with college-tie colors. Better yet is the library, all dark paneling, books, and a bar pouring drinks – a college don's dream study really

CHAPTER NINE: AMAZING FOOD ONE CAN FIND IN ENGLAND

Sunday Roast

A tradition if there ever was one. The Sunday roast meal is the quickest way to escape the gloom that comes with the end of the weekend. One of the most popular UK meals, the cornerstone of the wonderful dinner, is meat.

A typical roast supper will feature either lamb, roast beef, chicken, or turkey. If you're eating out, you may even have numerous. The beef is then served with a rich sauce and accompanied by roasted potatoes, cauliflower cheese, and Yorkshire Pudding. While a range of other condiments is added according to the meat, such as a mint sauce with pork. The Sunday roast meal is a defining aspect of British food and culture. It's a coming together of the family that has been a weekly event for generations.

Fish And Chips

British cuisine fish and Chips

Other regions of the Commonwealth have their take on what defines traditional fish and chips, but you can trace the roots clear to London. In 1860, the city built the first fish and chips business marking the commencement of the most genuine British dish.

Traditionally eaten with chunky chips (fries) and white fish such as haddock, fish, and chips is a daily element of British society. When the skies are ominous and the temperatures are low, the national cuisine is the ideal companion. Smothered in salt and vinegar and covered in newspaper, the chips are allowed to simmer while they wait for prying hands. Alongside the hefty dinner, you'll discover pickled onions and mushy peas. This recipe makes it simple to create at home. Make sure to also get a deep-fried mars bar for dessert!

Shepherd's Pie

The boundary between pie and, well, not a pie is a hazy one in UK's culinary culture. One of the greatest classic British dishes is Shepherd's Pie. While it isn't exactly a pie, it is a hearty supper.

You can find Shepherd's Pie throughout the UK. It started its climb to fame in Scotland when it was wrapped with pastry. From its ancient beginnings, the pie subsequently lost its shell in Ireland and was replaced with potato. The pie begins at the base, with a layer of chopped or minced lamb. The beef is then coated with onions, and an array of chopped vegetables and covered with a thick layer of mashed potato. After baking the pie, you're left with a substantial and delectable meal that will ease the winter blues.

Switch the lamb for beef to create a Cottage Pie instead or pork for Pork Pie. This is the greatest method to cook Shepherd's Pie!

Bread And Butter Pudding

You may be picking a trend with British meals. Heart-warming and nutritious, most of the traditional British foods serve to offset their persistently cold weather. Not that we should complain. After all, it gave us Bread and Butter Pudding.

The classic British meal goes back to medieval times when the pudding was prepared from bone marrow. Thankfully, the meal has altered throughout the decades. Now, bread is sliced and buttered before forming the basis of the wonderful dessert. After covering the foundation with currants and raisins, the bread is coated with egg custard. Bake until the buttered bread is brown and crisp for a delightful post-dinner treat.

Sticky Toffee Pudding

Indulging in Sticky Toffee Pudding is something everyone must do while in the UK. The iconic British dessert is one you'll be eager to prepare back home. Thankfully, you'll find everything you need at your local grocery. The pudding is simply a sponge cake that is slathered with melted toffee, giving a thick and sticky texture. It's sweet and delightful at worst and tantalizing at its finest. To complement the hot dessert, add a side of custard or ice cream, which will melt in contact with the hot toffee.Yorkshire Pudding

Yorkshire Pudding

A popular British meal that you'll usually find with your Sunday roast, Yorkshire Pudding, is not your normal pudding. Far from a sweet treat, the pudding is a savory pastry whose roots trace back to the mid-1700s.

Instead of custard or sticky toffee, the pudding is caked with gravy and served as an appetizer. This hearty beginning was included since the main meal would frequently be too little. Now, in more contemporary and gluttonous times, the Yorkshire Pudding survives as the companion for the meat.

Baking the pudding at home will take a few attempts to perfect, but adds an additional layer to your roast, or any of your favorite winter recipes.

Toad In The Hole

If you're wondering what ways you may integrate Yorkshire Pudding in additional recipes, then the Toad in the Hole may be the classic British delicacy you're hunting for. The name may be off-putting, but don't worry, no toads were hurt in the production of this meal.

Using the pudding, the interior is filled with meat. The meat of choice was often offal, pigeon, or steak. The pudding and meat are then cooked at the same time, causing the flesh to rise to the top, like floating toads.

While this meal was employed to further the scant meat supply in the poorest regions, it blossomed into a popular dish that's now offered across the UK. Pork sausages are now the traditional protein element, with many eateries taking liberties and adding their own flavor to the dish.

Lancashire Hot Pot

Many of us may relate to the predicament of Lancashire women in the late 1800s. With the local cotton industry prospering, many went to work, leaving little time at the end of the day to prepare. This is a typical concern for many of us in the 21st century. Their answer was the Lancashire Hot Pot.

The slow cook meal is the best alternative for anybody seeking to return home with a great supper ready to be served. The hot pot features lamb (mutton in earlier times), a mix of chopped vegetables topped with a layer of thinly sliced potatoes.

Left in a high-rise dish to cook during the day, the women of Lancashire were able to come home to a full lunch. You can too if you attempt it from this recipe.

Pie, Mash & Liquor

Around the same time as the fish and chips fad spread throughout the UK, the original Pie, Mash, and Liquor were gaining favor in central London. The original dish was formed of eels that lived in vast quantities near the filthy River Thames. The eels were incorporated into a pie and served with mashed potato.

As for the liquor component, well, it was generated from the eels but doesn't contain an ounce of alcohol. As better meats were freely accessible, the Eel Pie, Mash, and

Liquor dropped out of favor until minced beef replaced the fish.

Since then, it has grown to be one of the most popular British delicacies and is coated with a tasty but unattractive green sauce created from spices and parsley. If you still want to taste eels whilst in London, jellied eels are widely available at the city's pie and mash businesses.

Scones

Found at every afternoon tea throughout the UK, scones are a fluffy, sweet bread with a crunchy surface. The dish harks back to the 1500s in Scotland. But it was the Duchess of Bedford who prompted scones to become so famous and a requirement with your afternoon cup of tea.

She would regularly feel hungry at about 4 pm, and one day begged for some sweet pastries. Scones were put on her dish, initiating her own infatuation, and soon the country followed. Scones come in a range of flavors, some savory, and some sweet. But the scones in southern England are legendary. Here you may have your afternoon tea with a scone, clotted cream, and strawberry jam. Now, if only we could all agree on one pronunciation.

Steak And Kidney Pudding or Pie

Also called Steak and Kidney Pie (because it truly is a pie), this classic British cuisine is a frequent lunch order across the United Kingdom. The suet pastry is delectable owing to its buttery and flaky flavor. The interior is a blast of heated gravy, steak, and kidney (from pig or sheep) together with lots of chopped onions.

The steak and kidney pudding are often served over mashed potatoes, beans, and an extra layer of gravy. The meat-centric lunch is guaranteed to be hearty, but when paired with a cool brew, you'll feel like you fully understand local cuisine.

Deep Fried Mars Bars

If you're roaming about the UK and develop a yearning for a warm sweet treat, then make a beeline for your local fish and chip shop. A popular menu item with your haddocks and fries is the deep-fried Mars bar.

You won't find this dessert on the healthy eating pyramid, but its sweet richness is beyond delectable. A deep-fried Mars bar is first caked in batter (beer is sometimes used) and then dipped into the scorching oil, sealing up all the sweetness and creating a crispy exterior.

Part crunchy doughnut, part delicious chocolate bar, the deep-fried Mars bar will give you that sugar boost to go on your excursions.

Full English Breakfast

One typical British cuisine you might have come across before is the full English breakfast. Served across the globe, you still can't top the original. Just be prepared for an amazing cooked breakfast feast that will tie you over well into midday.

Comprising eggs as you want them, baked beans, bacon, mushrooms, tomatoes, and fried bread, it's little surprise why they call the Full English Breakfast a fry-up. It's been reproduced but not duplicated, and there's no better way to start your morning.

The simplicity of the recipe, however, makes it one of the greatest UK foods to attempt at home. While traveling across the UK, you'll encounter distinct twists depending on the nation you're in.

Black Pudding

Commonly featured on the Full English Breakfast Plate, Black Pudding is a divisive yet typical British delicacy. The dish is similar to a sausage but is produced with blood blended with a mixer such as oats. After a time, they coagulate.

Black Pudding has been around for millennia, with evidence linking it to the 4th century. From the days of Roman colonization until today, the dish has remained contentious, particularly among certain religious groups.

You'll either love it or loathe it, but as you travel throughout the UK, give it a chance to enjoy one of the oldest British meals.

Bangers And Mash

Hot and hearty comfort meals make up the majority of the local cuisine. This is perhaps why pub culture is so prevalent in the United Kingdom. You'll find several of these foods on the pub menu, with a long-time mainstay being Bangers & Mash. Simple and tasty, Bangers & Mash is a classic working-class dinner. The dish comprises British sausage (precise variety varies everywhere you go) and, of course, mashed potatoes served with a substantial helping of gravy, veggies, and frequently baked beans.

A fantastic example of a British colloquialism is the phrase banger. At no other time is the phrase used to describe a sausage. So be careful never to order a sausage and mash.

Bacon Sandwich

From the most contentious of traditional foods to something virtually everyone can get behind, the Bacon Sandwich is as good and straightforward as it sounds.

The sandwich is a frequent morning meal. Being so straightforward, it's easy to cook at home if you're in haste, while take-out establishments will have it ready in no time. The bread is frequently sliced thick, with sourdough being a delightful alternative. While the rasher bacon is barely cooked, making it simple to chew.

Chosen condiments may vary in flavor with tomato or Worcestershire sauce, a common option. If you have time, add some arugula and mozzarella cheese.

Scotch Egg

Scotch Egg is a much-loved yet unusual meal that's popular at neighborhood picnics. The egg is first hard-boiled before being wrapped with sausage meat and deep-fried.

The sausage meat is normally formed with minced pork and coated with herbs, spices, and breadcrumbs. Once the food is cooking, wait until it becomes golden brown and has a crispy outside. From then it is stored in the fridge to later be served cold. If you've been invited to a picnic in the park by your UK buddies, bring along some Scotch Eggs to show off your knowledge of local cuisine.

Jam Roly Poly

Through the majority of the 1900s, Jam Roly Poly was a welcome appearance at an after-school meal. The exquisite delicacy has a shorter history than many British cuisines on our list, but Jam Roly Poly is regarded in great favor.

The dish is simple and straightforward to create from your own home. The "stodgy" dish is prepared from dough made from suet and topped with strawberry jam. Afterward, the dough is coiled up before being cooked or steamed. Once the dessert is ready to be served, put on a substantial dollop of hot custard (and more jam if you desire) for a wonderful blast of warm flavor.

Cullen Skink

Although a touch harsh on the ears, Cullen Skink tastes a lot nicer than it sounds. Originating in Cullen, a little village on the northeast coast of Scotland, Cullen Skink soon spread over the northern areas.

The soup immediately warms the body and soul, a part of what made it so popular throughout the long Scottish winters. Back then, the fish soup was prepared with cold-smoked haddock known as Finnan Haddie. Now you'll discover all varieties of haddock that are employed, accompanied by a tasty broth.

The best way to sample Cullen Skink is in Scotland since it seldom occurs on menus elsewhere in the UK.

Christmas Pudding

Alongside Trifle, Christmas Pudding is a favorite dessert post-Christmas dinner. After having all the trappings of a great feast, with lots of Shepherd's Pie and Sausage Rolls, the country returns to the table to savor a delicious blend of fruit, spices, and a splash of alcohol.

Christmas Pudding initially appeared on local dishes back in the 14th century. Back then, it also featured mutton and beef, reducing its appeal. It was transformed into what we know today a few decades later before being prohibited by Puritans. 70 years later, King George uplifted the prohibition, enabling the public to once again enjoy the Christmas treat.

To prepare it at home, you'll need to soak stale bread in milk before adding candied citron, nutmeg, eggs, raisin, and, significantly, brandy before boiling. Serve with whipped cream.

Vegetarian British Cuisine

With so much traditional British cuisine containing meat-centric dishes, you'd be excused for believing that the UK would be tough for vegetarian and vegan tourists. Thankfully, this is not the case.

The vegetarian movement in the United Kingdom truly has a specific beginning point. Cranks, a restaurant in west London, championed the trend in the 1960s, bringing a spectrum of wonderful vegetarian meals and variations on conventional food to our plates.

It's simple to sample some of the greatest recipes on this list using vegetarian equivalents such as tofu or tempeh. While true ethnic food, notably Indian is easily accessible across the UK.

CHAPTER TEN: WHY YOU NEED TO VISIT ENGLAND

Despite its tiny size, England possesses a mind-boggling diversity of natural marvels, cities, historical sites, and more. It is brimming with distinct cultures, languages, and places. From the busy city of London to the picturesque coastline of Cornwall and the rolling hills of the Peak District.

London

We have to start with the capital — the big smoke, London. This is the primary financial, economic, and governmental area of the nation and everything occurs here. It is the residence of the royal family, of parliament, and many historic events have taken place here.

Not only that, but London is also a fantastic city to visit. It is crammed with ancient buildings, lovely parks, and contemporary attractions. Examples include the Tower of London, the Tower Bridge, Buckingham Palace, The Shard, Big Ben and the Houses of Parliament, and the London Eye. You might easily spend a week in London and yet not see everything it has to offer.

Stonehenge

Deep in the heart of southwest England in the town of Salisbury, you may discover the epic stone circle of Stonehenge. This is frequently one of the key reasons to visit England after tourists have seen the capital. It enjoys international renown and welcomes swarms of visitors year-round.

Stonehenge is an old, prehistoric stone circle that continues to fascinate scientists and archaeologists until this day. The stone columns tower tall and have an astounding weight. This has caused some to ponder how it was created since, at the time, mankind had no lifting technology or specialized tools. It is a sight to view, especially at dawn and sunset. Furthermore, the adjoining Stonehenge Museum is crammed with intriguing exhibits and history.

York

The Shambles in York

York is one of the most popular cities in North Yorkshire owing to its attractiveness and history. It is also a fantastic area to stay if you wish to see Yorkshire and the North Yorkshire Moors.

One of the major reasons to visit England and York is the castle and walls. The medieval walls encompass most of the city and you may still wander on the ramparts. The JORVIK Viking Centre is also wonderful and provides you with a genuine insight into what life under Viking control would have been like with the noises and smells!

Oxford

Together with Cambridge, Oxford is the other prominent university city in England. These two educational institutions provide the highest levels of study in the nation. While the university is renowned, Oxford is also a wonderful town to visit.

The river Thames flows through it, and it boasts some wonderful architecture, museums, and landmarks. The many colleges and their historic architecture are amazing to see, but other buildings like the circular Radcliffe Cinema and the Bridge of Sighs are just as spectacular. We also propose a trip to the Oxford University Museum of Natural History which has some amazing exhibits, exhibitions, and specimens.

Jurassic Coast

The amazing Durdle Door on the Jurassic Coast

Dorset is located in the southwest of England and is a wonderful section of the nation to explore. It is perfect for camping and caravanning trips. Possibly one of the most popular sites within this region is the Jurassic Coast. This is a World Heritage site that runs from Exmouth to Studland Bay.

It is defined by epic cliffs that have eroded through time to reveal ancient rock formations from the Jurassic, Triassic, and Cretaceous eras. As a consequence, numerous fossilized remnants of creatures have been uncovered including dinosaurs.

The coastline is fantastic and there are also some great walking paths and stunning beaches. One of the most renowned attractions here, though, is the beautiful Durdle Door. This is a natural rock archway that juts out into the sea and provides some spectacular sunsets.

Cambridge

Cambridge is arguably the best-known university city jointly with Oxford and it is a terrific destination to visit. It is situated to the north of London and has significant transport connectivity on the M11. Indeed, you could simply organize a day excursion from the capital if you wished to see this attractive and ancient city.

Cambridge is arguably best known for its university but it also boasts some amazing buildings and gardens. Possibly the most popular is the King's College Chapel. This historic edifice stands near the banks of the river Cam and it is here that the world-famous King's College Choir performs and polishes their ability. Cambridge also offers numerous wonderful museums like the University Museum of Zoology and the Museum of Archaeology and Anthropology.

Bath

Traditional architecture in Bath

If you want to explore a portion of England that has ties to ancient Rome, we propose a trip to Bath. As you might think, this city is famed for its Roman bathhouses and you may explore some of the historic remnants.

Furthermore, Bath is jam-packed with wonderful and historic architecture. Examples include Bath Abbey, the Royal Crescent the Guildhall, and Pulteney Bridge. If you are visiting Somerset and want a day excursion, Bath is highly recommended. Aside from the amazing architecture and history, the city is also quite lovely also with the river Avon flowing straight through it to offer some delightful waterside vistas.

St Ives

The lovely beaches of St. Ives in Cornwall

St Ives is the archetypal Cornish coastal town and is one of the most popular attractions in the region. It is endowed with three magnificent beaches, but also boasts attractive architecture, and some outstanding sites like the Tate Museum, and the harbor.

If you want a typical Cornish experience, this is the place to come. You may also indulge in a choice of water activities here, and just a short drive or walk, there is also the huge Hayle Beach and golden sands that spread for miles along St Ives Bay.

Lake District

High up in the northwest of England, below the Scottish border, you may explore the magnificent Lake District. This national park and area is recognized for its beauty and is generally regarded as one of the most gorgeous spots in the country.

The Lake District is made up of several hills, mountains, and of course lakes. Some of the big lakes are Windemere, Buttermere, Grasmere, and Ullswater. These huge bodies of water are genuinely stunning and surrounded by breathtaking landscapes, and quaint villages like Bowness on Windemere.

If you enjoy hiking and boating and want to discover the English landscape that poets have written about, go no farther than the Lake District.

Brighton

If you want a real English beach experience whilst visiting London, Brighton is a terrific spot to come to. From the capital, it is around a 2-hour trip. However, there is also a direct train route connecting the two towns and the travel is affordable and takes little over an hour.

Brighton is a coastal town and hence boasts all the classic joys you may imagine - ice cream, fish and chips, arcades, and a long length of golden beach. Brighton Pier is another must-see destination and you can stroll down the length of the pier and visit the theme park at the end equipped with roller coasters and attractions. Don't forget to check out the remnants of the renowned west pier too that still exist in the sea and reflect a bygone age of Victorian Brighton.

Peak District

The Peak District is possibly the most stunning natural location in England next to the Lake District. I personally prefer the Peak District, although I live within a short drive from there and have spent many days exploring the region.

This National Park is situated in central England in Derbyshire and Yorkshire. The beauty here is spectacular and you can expect to witness rolling hills, green valleys, and craggy peaks. There are so many locations to visit in the Peak District that it is impossible to identify them all. Popular examples include Dovedale, Ladybower Reservoir, Stanage Edge, the High Peaks, Kinder Scout, and Monsal Head Viaduct. If you want to explore the natural treasures of the nation, the Peak District is one of the top reasons to visit England.

Glastonbury

If you visit Stonehenge, it is not impractical to also take a day trip to Glastonbury. This picturesque village is notable for several reasons and is a fascinating destination. Primarily, it is renowned for the iconic Glastonbury music festival where musicians like David Bowie, Bruce Springsteen, and Metallica have made their imprint.

However, the town of Glastonbury is also steeped in myth and English folklore. It has associations with King Arthur, the knights of the round table, and Merlin. There are also crusader linkages and stories about the mythical Holy Grail that bloom here. You will find the town extremely intriguing, and we highly suggest hiking to the top of Glastonbury Tor for magnificent views of the southwest countryside.

Whitby

The east coast of England is home to several wonderful coastal communities like Mablethorpe, Skegness, and Scarborough.

However, Whitby is one that sticks out and has a wholly distinct character and charm.

Whitby is situated farther north, at the edge of the magnificent North Yorkshire Moors. It is a small town that is overflowing with history and provides a wonderful combination of classic English beach activities, coupled with ancient buildings.

On one cliff, you may climb the 200 stairs to witness the remnants of Whitby Abbey. Alternatively, why not stroll down to the waterfront and walk along the embracing arms of the two harbor walls? Don't forget to sample some fish and chips at Magpie Café, spend some pennies in the arcades, or take a stroll on the west bank beach.

Forest of Dean

If you want to explore one of the surviving historic forests in England, a visit to the Forest of Dean is an essential must. This region encompasses around 110 square km and was originally a royal crown forest where hunting was authorized.

Located near the Welsh border and the River Wye, the Forest of Dean features miles of walking routes that weave through these beautiful woods. If you enjoy hiking and immersing yourself in nature, this location will be a treasure trove.

Norfolk Broads

If you go to the east of England into Norfolk, you may explore the huge river network and marshes that is the Norfolk Broads. This area is surrounded by magnificent fens and boasts miles and miles of tranquil canals, rivers, and waterways.

As it is one of the flattest locations in the UK, the Broads is great for boating. Indeed, many UK residents charter boats and spend a week or two of delightful sailing on the waterways. You may rent contemporary boats or even historic canal boats. The experience is like nothing other, and the rivers are dotted with numerous typical English pubs and places to explore.

Liverpool

A monument of the Beatles in Liverpool

Liverpudlians are a breed unto themselves and many people visit this section of the nation solely to hear the peculiar Scouse dialect. However, Liverpool City is also a fantastic location and one of the top reasons to visit England.

It has a lovely riverfront position against the background of the river Mersey, and if you can sail along this canal, the Liverpool docks are really striking. Aside from that, Liverpool offers some fantastic sights such as the Maritime Museum, the Titanic Memorial, and the famed Cavern Club where the iconic English rock and roll band The Beatles once played. Indeed, you cannot avoid the fab four while visiting Liverpool and The Beatles Story is well worth a visit too, even if you aren't an obsessive fan.

Yorkshire Dales

The Yorkshire Dales is another magnificent National Park and one of the biggest in England. It stands below the Lake District, but above the Peak District and is on the verge of both Leeds and Manchester. The Dales is home to the highest mountain in England — Ingleborough, combined with other formidable peaks like Pen-y-Ghent, and Skiddaw.

Aside from the opportunity for dramatic mountain excursions, the Yorkshire Dales also features some beautiful vistas and landmarks. For example, you may visit the Ribble Valley and view the huge industrial revolution architecture of Ribblehead Viaduct or walk to the top of Malham Cove to see where several scenes from Harry Potter and the Deathly Hallows were shot.

Lindisfarne

England has had a stormy history in which it has been attacked and conquered several times by the Vikings and of course, William the Conqueror. During this history, one site has stayed staunch and served as a beacon of English faith and culture — that spot is Lindisfarne and is one of the top reasons to visit England.

The Holy Island as it is often called is in Northumbria and has a history extending back to the 6th century AD and is one of the most significant places of Christianity in the UK. It is a great spot to visit and is only accessible by a road that is buried by tidal water for much of the day. On the island, you may visit Lindisfarne Castle, many lighthouses, and also the harsh nature reserve.

the Isle of Wight

The Isle of Wight is located off of the southern coast of England immediately below Southampton and Portsmouth. It is just a short boat trip from Southampton and is an intriguing destination to explore. Despite being part of England, the island has its own culture and customs, and it delivers a distinct experience.

The Needles is a must-see natural feature on the western coast of the Isle of Wight near Yarmouth. This is a collection of chalkstone rock stacks that jut out into the water. What's worse, is that someday these rocks will simply disintegrate into the river and be lost to time. A visit to Alum Bay is also highly recommended since here the cliffs offer a beautiful assortment of various colored sand ranging from red and yellow, to purple, and orange.

Land's End

Land's End in Cornwall

Cornwall has some gorgeous, craggy coasts and it is one of the most popular vacation destinations for UK citizens. This is owing to the aforementioned shoreline, the stunning beaches, the easygoing lifestyle, and tiny fishing villages and coastal towns.

One of the most popular sights here is Land's End. Located in Penzance, Land's End is literally the most southwestern point in England. Go much farther, and you are having a bath in the Celtic Sea! The seaside environment here is spectacular and dramatic. The craggy cliffs are pounded by the sea, and you may see hundreds of seagulls too. Don't forget to have a Cornish Pasty here or sample some wonderful and fatty clotted cream ice cream!